CHRIS HANNAN

Chris Hannan's work has been produced by the Royal Shakespeare Company and by Sir Peter Hall at the Old Vic. *The Evil Doers* won a Time Out Award and the Charrington London Fringe Best Play Award when first seen at the Bush Theatre, and he was nominated Lloyds Bank Playwright of the Year for *Shining Souls* in 1996. Five of his plays have premiered at the Traverse Theatre, Edinburgh, including the contemporary classic *Elizabeth Gordon Quinn,* which was revived by the National Theatre of Scotland in its inaugural 2006 season. His 2010 play for children and families *The Three Musketeers and the Princess of Spain* won five star reviews in England and a Scottish Critics' CATS Award for Best New Play. *The God of Soho*, commissioned for Shakespeare's Globe, premiered there in 2011.

His debut novel *Missy* was awarded the 2009 McKitterick Prize by the Society of Authors.

Other Titles in this Series

Howard Brenton
ANNE BOLEYN
BERLIN BERTIE
FAUST – PARTS ONE & TWO
    after Goethe
IN EXTREMIS
NEVER SO GOOD
PAUL
THE RAGGED TROUSERED
    PHILANTHROPISTS
    after Tressell

Caryl Churchill
BLUE HEART
CHURCHILL PLAYS: THREE
CHURCHILL PLAYS: FOUR
CHURCHILL: SHORTS
CLOUD NINE
A DREAM PLAY
    after Strindberg
DRUNK ENOUGH TO SAY
    I LOVE YOU?
FAR AWAY
HOTEL
ICECREAM
LIGHT SHINING IN
    BUCKINGHAMSHIRE
MAD FOREST
A NUMBER
SEVEN JEWISH CHILDREN
THE SKRIKER
THIS IS A CHAIR
THYESTES *after* Seneca
TRAPS

Ariel Dorfman
DEATH AND THE MAIDEN
PURGATORIO
READER
THE RESISTANCE TRILOGY
WIDOWS

Helen Edmundson
ANNA KARENINA *after* Tolstoy
THE CLEARING
CORAM BOY *after* Gavin
GONE TO EARTH *after* Webb
LIFE IS A DREAM *after* Calderón
THE MILL ON THE FLOSS
    after Eliot
MOTHER TERESA IS DEAD
ORESTES *after* Euripides
WAR AND PEACE *after* Tolstoy

Debbie Tucker Green
BORN BAD
DIRTY BUTTERFLY
RANDOM
STONING MARY
TRADE & GENERATIONS
TRUTH AND RECONCILIATION

Chris Hannan
THE GOD OF SOHO
SHINING SOULS

Liz Lochhead
BLOOD AND ICE
DRACULA *after* Stoker
EDUCATING AGNES ('The School
    for Wives') *after* Molière
GOOD THINGS
MARY QUEEN OF SCOTS GOT
    HER HEAD CHOPPED OFF
MEDEA *after* Euripides
MISERYGUTS ('The Miser')
    & TARTUFFE *after* Molière
PERFECT DAYS
THEBANS *after* Euripides &
Sophocles

Linda McLean
ANY GIVEN DAY
ONE GOOD BEATING
RIDDANCE
SHIMMER
STRANGERS, BABIES

Joanna Murray-Smith
BOMBSHELLS
THE FEMALE OF THE SPECIES
HONOUR

Rona Munro
THE HOUSE OF BERNARDA ALBA
    after Lorca
THE INDIAN BOY
IRON
THE LAST WITCH
LITTLE EAGLES
LONG TIME DEAD
THE MAIDEN STONE
MARY BARTON *after* Gaskell
PANDAS
STRAWBERRIES IN JANUARY
    from de la Chenelière
YOUR TURN TO CLEAN THE
STAIR & FUGUE

Chris Hannan

ELIZABETH GORDON QUINN

NICK HERN BOOKS

London

www.nickhernbooks.co.uk

A Nick Hern Book

Elizabeth Gordon Quinn first published in Great Britain in 1990 by Nick Hern Books Limited, 14 Larden Road, London W3 7ST in the anthology *Scot-Free*

This revised edition published in 2006 in association with the National Theatre of Scotland

Reprinted 2011

Elizabeth Gordon Quinn copyright © 1990, 2006 Chris Hannan

Chris Hannan has asserted his right to be identified as the author of this work

Cover design by Freight Design

Typeset by Country Setting, Kingsdown, Kent, CT14 8ES
Printed and bound in Great Britain by CLE Print Ltd, St Ives, Cambs PE27 3LE

A CIP catalogue record for this book is available from the British Library

ISBN-13   978 1 85459 921 6

This revised version of *Elizabeth Gordon Quinn* was first performed at Dundee Rep Theatre on 27 April 2006, with the following cast:

WILLIAM QUINN	Billy McColl
ELIZABETH GORDON QUINN	Cara Kelly
SPECIAL BRANCH OFFICER/ SHERRIFF'S OFFICER/ COALMAN/RSM	John Ramage
MAURA QUINN	Lesley Hart
MRS BLACK	Myra McFadyen
MRS CUNNINGHAM	Pauline Goldsmith
DOLAN/BROGAN/ SERGEANT	Antony Strachan
HAGGERTY/ McCORQUONDALE	John Kielty
AIDAN QUINN	Robin Laing

Director	John Tiffany
Designer	Neil Warmington
Composer and Sound Designer	David Paul Jones
Lighting Designer	Chahine Yavroyan

For my father

John Hannan
(1924-1993)

*boilermaker, salesman
and biographer of John Wheatley*

Characters

ELIZABETH GORDON QUINN
WILLIAM QUINN
MAURA QUINN
AIDAN QUINN

MRS BLACK
MRS CUNNINGHAM
MARTIN BROGAN
PETE McCORQUONDALE

SPECIAL BRANCH OFFICER
SHERIFF'S OFFICER
DOLAN
HAGGERTY
SERGEANT
REGIMENTAL SERGEANT-MAJOR

CRIPPLED SOLDIER
PASSERS-BY

The play is set in Glasgow in 1915.

ACT ONE

*A kitchen dominated by the presence of a large piano. This
should look rather splendid, of course, but out of place. Dirty
kitchen pots full of water sit on top of it; and above it there's a
pulley on which clothes are hanging. On the floor, patches of
newspaper have been laid in place of linoleum; and there are
areas of sawdust where something has been spilled. There is a
bed recess curtained off by a sheet hung up on a rope. The rest
of the kitchen might be sketchy but perhaps a range for
cooking and a sink – basically, there needs to be enough
'kitchen-sink' for us to see the act of will and imagination that
is required to raise oneself above such things – and believe
oneself to be in a space which contains nothing but a striking-
looking piano and oneself.*

*But it would give the audience a misleading impression if the
set suggested social realism. There might be elements that are
wholly open about the set's theatricality – missing or
incomplete walls, for instance – and the set overall should
have a metaphysical quality. Above and beyond the kitchen,
the common stair of the tenement rises to a half-landing where
it ends in a black and lonely void. I see it as an image from
some Inferno, this stairway, a lonely lonely place where Dante
might punish those who prefer their own imagination to the
society of others.*

Scene One

*The play begins with some to-ings and fro-ings on the street
outside and the tenement stair. Maybe we see* MRS
CUNNINGHAM, *a munitions worker, set off to work. Maybe,
to establish the war, we see a* CRIPPLED SOLDIER *amusing
himself with a mouth organ.*

A SPECIAL BRANCH OFFICER *enters and takes in the scene. Then he stops* MRS BLACK, *who is returning home with a pram-ful of washing, and asks her about the Quinns, how many of them there are and exactly which flat they live in. She points it out and continues on her way. The* SPECIAL BRANCH OFFICER *watches the house.*

In the kitchen, WILLIAM QUINN *is playing with a quiz (now called a yo-yo). As the lights begin to focus our attention on the kitchen – and away from the outside –* WILLIAM *begins to act in a secretive and stealthy manner. First he checks that his wife, who has gone next door, is occupied. Then he cautiously opens up the inside of the piano and finds a half-bottle of whisky which he has hidden in the innards. As he takes a sip, the* SPECIAL BRANCH OFFICER *knocks at the door of our room-and-kitchen house. Very loud. As* WILLIAM *gets a scare and hides the bottle,* ELIZABETH *enters.*

WILLIAM. Who can that be?

ELIZABETH. Sounds like the police. Have you done something untoward again?

WILLIAM. No.

ELIZABETH. Then open the door.

WILLIAM. No. You know the police, they're a thesaurus of errors.

More knocking.

ELIZABETH. It's too hot to *do* anything, they can pass the time.

WILLIAM *opens the door. The* SPECIAL BRANCH OFFICER *comes in.*

OFFICER (*Ulster accent*). Special Branch.

ELIZABETH. Come in, Officer. If we can be of any assistance to the country in this time of war and peril, you will find us to the front.

OFFICER. You're Mrs Quinn, are you?

ELIZABETH. I am.

OFFICER. You won't mind if I'm rude? I wouldn't be doing my job if I didn't snoop around a little.

Watching where he puts his feet, the SPECIAL BRANCH OFFICER *has a look around. He looks into the room off.*

WILLIAM. In this tenement we are of course adjacent to the notorious shipyards.

OFFICER. Indeed.

WILLIAM. We hear criticism of the government which is unmusical in the extreme.

OFFICER (*picks up a book*). Ah. Dante's *Inferno*.

ELIZABETH. Yes; after a day of grim reality, Dante's vision of hell cheers us up.

OFFICER (*looking around the kitchen*). I've seen worse.

ELIZABETH. The grim reality I'm referring to is the shortage of piano recitals in this district and the absence of like minds.

OFFICER. You have a son. Aidan Quinn. He volunteered for service with the Sixth Royal Munsters, currently seeing action in the Dardanelles.

ELIZABETH. Yes.

OFFICER. He deserted. He went missing in Dublin before his regiment embarked for Turkey. The least ridiculous hypothesis is that he's dead.

WILLIAM. Dead?

OFFICER. Unless he's being sheltered.

He points to a statue of the Infant of Prague or similar.

You're Roman Catholics, I see.

WILLIAM. Yes.

OFFICER. What Irish connections do you have, Mr Quinn?

ELIZABETH. Not all Catholics in Scotland are of Irish origin, Officer.

WILLIAM. My wife's maiden name is Gordon. Elizabeth Gordon Quinn.

ELIZABETH. The Gordons are Scots Catholics, as are some of our oldest and finest families. You will have heard of the Crichton-Stuarts, personal and, I might add, very dear friends of mine.

OFFICER. And you, Mr Quinn, you have no Irish connections?

ELIZABETH. Mr Quinn is a civil servant.

OFFICER. It's your day off, I see.

ELIZABETH. He was a civil servant. The Irish are like drunks; they suffer from the great delusion that they have no delusions about themselves.

OFFICER. Did your son know of your antipathy towards the Irish?

No answer.

Yet of all the regiments in the British army, he joined the Royal Munsters, an Irish regiment. Why? – Did he do it to spite you? – Does he have Fenian sympathies?

ELIZABETH. He has no sympathies of any kind.

OFFICER. Whereabouts in Ireland do your people come from, Mr Quinn?

WILLIAM. My father was an orphan, he was brought up in a Home somewhere near Belfast.

OFFICER. When he came to Scotland he left behind no family at all?

WILLIAM. He often complained there was nobody in all Ireland that he could even write to.

OFFICER. I see. – Is it likely your son would want to come home?

ELIZABETH. I hope he would know us better than to expect a welcome.

OFFICER. Well, he may get desperate. If he does, then mark my words: harbouring deserters is a crime. Some of us no longer have sons to harbour, only in our hearts.

The SPECIAL BRANCH OFFICER *leaves.*

ELIZABETH. Don't say a word about this to his sister.

WILLIAM. I won't.

ELIZABETH. I don't want to hear it spoken of.

ELIZABETH *goes to exit to her bedroom. But stops.*

ELIZABETH. Where exactly in hell does Dante put traitors?

WILLIAM. The lowest circle.

ELIZABETH. What torment do they suffer?

WILLIAM. They freeze.

ELIZABETH. Good.

Scene Two

WILLIAM*'s shaving with a basin of hot water and a mirror placed on a table or the floor. He's a little tipsy.* MAURA *enters.*

WILLIAM. Maura, what are you doing home at this time?

MAURA. It's my lunch hour. I bought some bones out the butcher's to make soup for tonight. How are you?

WILLIAM. As happy as a pagan.

MAURA. I was at eight o'clock mass this morning.

WILLIAM. How often have I told you. The sort of man you are likely to meet at eight o'clock mass doesn't get married.

MAURA. I was talking to Jimmy Quinn the Latin teacher.

WILLIAM. Jimmy Quinn the Latin teacher has a passion for church music. I believe it's the purity of the boys' unbroken voices which appeals.

MAURA (*touched*). Awww. Anyway, he said there was a knock on the door first thing this morning and a Sheriff's Officer tried to serve him with a warrant for rent arrears. Said they were going to seize his belongings.

WILLIAM. A man like that has a disease of the mind. There are so many ways he could get into debt, I shudder to think.

MAURA. Jimmy showed them his rent book with all his payments up to date.

WILLIAM. A boy that can sing Palestrina's 'Missa Papae Marcelli' will like expensive ice cream; and toys, I shouldn't wonder. It was a mistake?

MAURA. Somehow or another they'd gone to the wrong address. The fella asked Jimmy Quinn were there any other Quinns in this street.

WILLIAM. And what did Jimmy Quinn say to that?

MAURA. He said yes, there was.

WILLIAM. And what did the filla say then?

MAURA. He told his men they'd have to go back and get a new warrant made out. I've been feeling nauseous all morning.

She picks up a letter she sees.

What's this here?

WILLIAM. Put that down.

MAURA. What is it?

WILLIAM. Down.

She puts it down.

It's a letter from the factor, notification of a forthcoming increase in rent.

MAURA. We're in arrears as it is.

WILLIAM. I know that.

MAURA. Maybe we should sell the piano.

WILLIAM. On you go back to work.

MAURA. It would be good for our sanity. She can't even play the thing.

WILLIAM. Watch what you say.

MAURA. I think we're all having a mental breakdown.

WILLIAM. Do you not get tired of saying that?

MAURA. I suppose I think that if I can say we're having a mental breakdown, then we can't be. Because if we were having a mental breakdown, we probably wouldn't know it.

ELIZABETH *enters*.

ELIZABETH. There's not a breath of air outside, it's like a baker's. Look at my flowers, like eager hearts.

MAURA. I bought some bones out the butcher's to make soup. Have you any money to buy some vegetables?

ELIZABETH (*indicating flowers*). What little money I had, Maura, I spent on these.

MAURA. What are we going to eat?

ELIZABETH. There's a tribe in New Guinea that eat their children.

MAURA. It's interesting. If a Sheriff's Officer came here to seize our belongings, would he find anything to make it worth his trouble, I wonder?

MAURA *goes*.

WILLIAM. We got a letter, Elizabeth.

ELIZABETH. Received. Got is not a word.

WILLIAM. Rent increases. We're in arrears as it is.

ELIZABETH. This is what happens when you lose your job, William.

WILLIAM. I agree I no longer have a position; I no longer have a position, I agree; all the more reason we should consider economies. Whether there is anything we might perhaps sell in order to relieve our debt.

He looks around to see if he might spy such a thing. There's not much in the room except a sink-ful of crap and a big piano.

ELIZABETH. I don't see anything. Do you?

WILLIAM. No, not right away. But maybe there's something we're overlooking because it's staring us in the face.

ELIZABETH. I'm prepared to sell our pots and pans if you think it'll help.

WILLIAM. How would we cook?

ELIZABETH. On dinner plates?

WILLIAM. I'm trying to imagine boiling a potato on a dinner plate.

ELIZABETH. I bought some music. Brahms' Rhapsody in B Minor.

WILLIAM. Anything else we might sell? Only I'm very much conscious we could be evicted due to these arrears, and I'm not sure I could stand to see you flung out on the streets, Elizabeth, or how you would bear it.

ELIZABETH. No, and I couldn't stand to see you dying of shame, William, to have brought your wife to such a sorry pass.

MRS BLACK *enters.*

MRS BLACK. These are dark times.

WILLIAM. Mrs Black, how are you?

MRS BLACK. Talk about depression? I've seen enough different shades of blackness to make a rainbow you could see at night. My days are filled with gloom and foreboding and in the evenings I've got my husband. Don't get me wrong: Mr Black's a good man but there are times a woman needs company. Any news of your son, Mrs Quinn?

ELIZABETH. It's the silence that's appalling.

MRS BLACK. The way the newspapers go quiet when there's a major new offensive.

WILLIAM. Your son's still missing, Mrs Black?

MRS BLACK. First we get word he's been wounded in France and he's been sent to hospital in England; then nothing. How can you lose a stretcher-case? It's not as if he could wander off.

WILLIAM. I'm sure your son isn't missing as such, Mrs Black, it's his papers which are missing. As a former civil servant, I can assure you he has most likely been mislaid.

MRS BLACK. Only a mother can know what it's like to be separated from her son. And as if life wasn't hellish enough, Mrs Cunningham is coming round the doors trying to stir up trouble. She wants to start a rent strike. She was talking to Mrs McManus downstairs and she turned to me and she says – O, here she is –

MRS CUNNINGHAM *enters. She's wearing her Sunday best, and has a Union Jack draped around her shoulders.*

– look at that, she's got the nerve to wrap herself in the Union Jack.

MRS CUNNINGHAM. The door was open, Mrs Quinn.

ELIZABETH. Come in, Mrs Cunningham; this is a tenement after all, we have no alternative but to enter into the spirit of things.

MRS CUNNINGHAM. You'll have received a letter regarding the rent increases.

MRS BLACK. Is one war not enough for you, you have to be starting another?

MRS CUNNINGHAM. There are two wars, you're right, Mrs Black, and in this war it's the landlords who are the Huns. The Tenants Defence Committee is asking all those affected by the increases to withhold rent. So far, over a hundred of us have signed this petition. The Committee will send it on to the factor, indicating that the proposed increases are not mutually agreed to. Read that, Mr Quinn; have I spelled all my words right? I was trying to write it in my best la-dee-dah English, I'd be obliged if you made any corrections.

WILLIAM. We couldn't just stop paying rent. Could we? We couldn't hope. I mean, we plural, we all of us, couldn't hope.

MRS CUNNINGHAM. The shipyard workers and munition workers have agreed to forego any wage rise for the duration of the war, why should there be any increase in rents? Of course it's worse for the wives of soldiers, they have to get by on separation allowances; and when they get behind with the rent, they're evicted, never mind their husbands are away fighting. All those who intend withholding rent will be asked to put up a Union Jack in their window along with a 'We Are Not Removing' poster. Mrs Black – will you sign?

MRS BLACK. I'm not one of these people who expect the earth, Mrs Cunningham.

MRS CUNNINGHAM (*taken aback, and unsure of her ground for a moment*). I'm surprised. We're doing this for the boys away at the war as much as anyone else. Mrs Quinn?

ELIZABETH. Are you asking me individually, Mrs Cunningham, or as a sliver of the working class? You and your kind seem to believe there is no such thing as the individual.

MRS CUNNINGHAM. You know what they say, Mrs Quinn. The individual dies, the species survives.

ELIZABETH. Are we supposed to be overjoyed about that?

MRS CUNNINGHAM. The things which are precious to us will carry on.

ELIZABETH. I won't know if they do or they don't. But what in any case is so precious about the species, if there is nothing wonderful about the individual?

MRS CUNNINGHAM. What is so precious about the individual that can't be found in every single one of them?

ELIZABETH. Genius?

MRS CUNNINGHAM. Mrs Quinn, you pay rent, I pay rent, the street pays rent; the landlord receives all our rents and pools it and spends that money as though his tenants were the same undivided person. If his tenants do not combine to act as an undivided person then they will not be a person of any description, each of them will be a piece of a body cut off from a hundred other pieces. So, Mrs Quinn, will you make us one whole person?

She offers ELIZABETH *the petition to sign.* ELIZABETH *takes it.*

ELIZABETH (*sitting on her piano stool*). I find myself in some difficulty, William. I don't wish to be ungracious; there may be others in the street less well-off than ourselves.

WILLIAM. You must, I'm sure, Mrs Cunningham, appreciate the difficulty of my wife's situation. The landlord is a personal and, I might add, very dear friend of ours; how public we could be in our support I just don't know.

The SHERIFF'S OFFICER *enters with two workmen –* DOLAN *and* HAGGERTY. *The* SHERIFF'S OFFICER *in suit and bowler hat,* DOLAN *and* HAGGERTY *in khaki overalls.* DOLAN *might have a protective arm around* HAGGERTY *because it's* HAGGERTY'*s first day on the job – and so he can explain things to him.* WILLIAM *– like everyone else – is entirely aware of their presence, but he decides to continue with what he's been saying and the* SHERIFF'S OFFICER *decides to wait until he's finished.*

It's something we would have to think long and hard about. I can of course see the material advantage that might accrue, but we have never been motivated by the desire for material gain, not when principles are at stake; and the idea of not paying rent is so opposite to our character and our philosophy that you will understand our mental – *are you three lost?*

SHERIFF'S OFFICER. We're looking for a Mr Quinn.

WILLIAM. Jimmy Quinn the Latin teacher?

SHERIFF'S OFFICER. William Quinn, formerly a civil servant, now dismissed. I'm the Sheriff's Officer. The court has granted the factor a warrant of sequestration which I've been appointed to execute.

He offers the warrant to WILLIAM, *who takes it.*

That warrant gives me the authority to seize any and all belongings appertaining to the household, in this case all belongings –

DOLAN. – notwithstanding we're not obliged to take the aforesaid belongings, if they're too clatty or for any other legal reason.

SHERIFF'S OFFICER. – though such belongings as we do seize –

DOLAN. – hereinafter known as the *invecta et illata* – ach, I'm going to night school –

SHERIFF'S OFFICER. – hereinafter known, to those of us not attending night school, as your stuff, which will then be held as security in respect of rent owing, interest on rent owing and current rent, and –

DOLAN (*to* HAGGERTY). – listen to this.

SHERIFF'S OFFICER. – expenses incurred by the actual sequestration.

DOLAN. They're paying for us. And not only are they paying so we can walk in and take their most treasured possessions, they're also paying so some charlie in a bowler hat can explain what we're going to do, before we go ahead and do it. Right, let's see how you get on. (*To all present.*) It's his first day. – You start over there, I'll start here. Stop, stop, stop. That's hopeless. You're walking like you're feart – which is understandable seeing as it's your first day – but you can't let them see you're feart. Watch, you need to walk a bit more gallus, think of an Orangeman on the Walk.

He demonstrates.

Right, now you try it.

HAGGERTY *tries to copy him.*

DOLAN. Aye; I'm a Catholic too. It's a bit unnatural at first. Right, imagine you've gone to confession and told the priest all the impure thoughts you've been having about your sister, and now you're walking home.

HAGGERTY *tries this new piece of direction and discovers
a more confident walk.*

Right, get stuck in.

HAGGERTY. Is this stuff worth anything?

DOLAN. The poor people might buy it.

HAGGERTY. Do the poor have much money?

DOLAN. Oodles.

MRS BLACK. Will we go, Mrs Quinn? Mrs Cunningham, will
we go?

WILLIAM. I'm sure there's an explanation for all this, Mrs
Black.

ELIZABETH. I cannot imagine what's happened, I'll call on
the factor tomorrow and discuss it with him in person.

WILLIAM. In the meantime will you put those things down –
put those things down – you can't just walk into our house
and trample over everything we hold most dear.

DOLAN (*to* HAGGERTY). See. Even in pitiful circumstances
like this you can still show your humanity. If you ignore
them it leaves them some dignity. Don't mistake what you
see for lack of sensitivity: I would like to weep – boo hoo
boo hoo, the human tragedy – what I do, I go home and
weep – that's the humanity of the man. Some nights the
tragedy of man can wring me dry.

SHERIFF'S OFFICER. This photograph is very impressive,
Mrs Quinn.

WILLIAM. You cannot take something as personal as a
photograph.

SHERIFF'S OFFICER. I'm afraid –

DOLAN. I'm afraid the factor can poind anything except in
point of fact personal clothing and the tools of your trade.
What is it he does?

SHERIFF'S OFFICER. He's a civil servant.

DOLAN (*to* WILLIAM). Here's a pencil, d'you want us to hunt for your mislaid file?

SHERIFF'S OFFICER. It's a fine-looking family. You must have opened your mouth a little as the photograph was taken, Mrs Quinn, it has blurred. The effect is bewitching.

WILLIAM. I fell in love with the photograph almost as much as with the real thing.

SHERIFF'S OFFICER. Your father is a striking-looking man, Mrs Quinn.

WILLIAM. I used always to say you could take him for a hussar, almost.

SHERIFF'S OFFICER. No 'almost', Mr Quinn. And what was he?

WILLIAM. He was employed by the Corporation.

SHERIFF'S OFFICER. As what?

ELIZABETH. Is it not enough you have walked into my house without permission, you also expect to strike up an acquaintance. He removed insanitary waste from communal toilets. He shovelled shite. The photograph was taken in a studio – what an illusion, what a grand illusion! Would you like to keep it as an aide-memoire; though you must meet so many types like us – characters.

SHERIFF'S OFFICER. I was only making small talk, Mrs Quinn.

DOLAN. He's got a habit of blundering into these things.

WILLIAM. Take the piano. Take everything.

SHERIFF'S OFFICER. That won't be necessary. – Dolan, leave the rest of the stoor, the piano is all we need.

WILLIAM (*angry, humiliated*). Can I help at all? Please direct me. You want help with the piano? Allow me, I insist.

DOLAN, HAGGERTY *and* WILLIAM *exit with the piano.*

SHERIFF'S OFFICER. Here's your photograph, Mrs Quinn.

ELIZABETH. It was only a cheap upright piano. No doubt we will obtain a better one.

The SHERIFF'S OFFICER *exits.*

MRS BLACK. O Mrs Quinn, those men walked into your house off the street as if you were nothing. Your house isn't as clean as most but you're still a woman.

MRS CUNNINGHAM. I'm sorry I saw this, Mrs Quinn. I wouldn't wish this on anyone. Do you think now you might join the rent strike?

ELIZABETH. In my opinion, Mrs Cunningham, your scheme somehow contrives to be both grandiose and squalid at the same time. I am not the working class: I am Elizabeth Gordon Quinn: and I have a right as an individual to pay rent to the factor if I so choose.

MRS CUNNINGHAM *exits, then* MRS BLACK. WILLIAM *re-enters.*

WILLIAM. Elizabeth, I admit there may have been moments when I wished the piano away. I promise I will do anything to get it back.

ELIZABETH *exits to the bedroom.* WILLIAM *is left to contemplate the empty space where the piano used to be.*

Scene Three

You know how when a picture is taken down from the wall you can see where it used to hang – you can see the empty space it used to occupy – well, if we could see the space where the piano used to be and feel its absence that would be an effect worth striving for. Maybe, for instance, the clutter that used to surround the piano could mark out the empty space it occupied – and the piano stool might remain where it has always been.

WILLIAM *is walking up and down, up and down.* ELIZABETH *enters from her bedroom.*

ELIZABETH. Please stop walking up and down. It's giving me a headache.

WILLIAM *stops walking up and down.*

Once I listened to Chopin mazurkas, Beethoven sonatas, Bach. Now all I hear is you walking up and down. The cacophony is hellish. – O, walk up and down if you want.

WILLIAM *returns to walking up and down.*

WILLIAM. The rent strike seems to be holding.

ELIZABETH. The success of a thing is not always a recommendation. You wouldn't recommend the flu.

WILLIAM. I might recommend studying the flu, if I was giving advice to other epidemics.

ELIZABETH. Vanity, vanity, all is vanity. The individual dies, the disease survives.

MAURA *enters, home from work. She places her wage packet on a chair – if there is a chair. Both* WILLIAM *and* ELIZABETH *are very aware of the wage packet.*

MAURA. There's my wages. By the time I got away from work it was too late to go shopping.

WILLIAM. So we've no food.

MAURA. No.

This doesn't need repeating or even bear repeating but WILLIAM *turns to* ELIZABETH *and says:*

WILLIAM. No food.

ELIZABETH. Without the piano this is an empty house. The piano was a living presence.

WILLIAM. I agree.

ELIZABETH. You agree that this is an empty house.

WILLIAM. Yes.

ELIZABETH. At least we're agreed on that.

MAURA. The pots aren't washed. She's had all day to wash the pots.

ELIZABETH. What's the point in washing pots when there's no food?

MAURA. It's not my fault there's no food. As a female post-office clerk I do not earn a fortune but the money might last the week if you didn't insist on paying the rent. You enjoy it. You dress up for it. It's a treat now to pay the rent.

WILLIAM. This is not producing food, Maura.

MAURA. A treat! Like the trout she buys.

WILLIAM. We can't eat wages.

ELIZABETH. Wages. We seem destined to earn nothing but wages in this household. It was always a bitter disappointment to me, Maura, that your father's particular grade of the civil service did not receive a salary.

ELIZABETH *picks up and pockets the wage packet.*

WILLIAM. There is a possibility the piano could be restored to us.

MAURA. Please no.

WILLIAM. The factor has to keep our belongings for a certain length of time before he can sell them. You see? I've been giving this matter some thought.

ELIZABETH. Do you have a suggestion?

WILLIAM. Mrs Cunningham.

ELIZABETH. Mrs Cunningham?

WILLIAM. You saw what happened to the factor's man when he came to deliver their notices to quit.

MAURA. The women threw everything at him.

WILLIAM. Flour. Soot. Worse.

ELIZABETH. How resourceful.

MAURA. Mrs Cunningham has certainly got them organised. She knows what she's doing.

ELIZABETH. Whereas I can't wash pots.

WILLIAM. The factor is as popular with them as the German Kaiser or the government. It's possible that if they were encouraged, they might go on the offensive – invade the factor's office and bring back the piano.

MAURA. Why would they do that?

WILLIAM. Why wouldn't they?

MAURA. Wouldn't they expect her to join the rent strike?

WILLIAM. They might expect her to express support.

MAURA. I could go and ask her if you like.

WILLIAM. Yes, go and tell Mrs Cunningham your mother would like to see her, please.

ELIZABETH. No 'please'.

WILLIAM. No 'please'. Just – your mother would like to see her.

MAURA *exits*.

We will have to think of a way to express our gratitude.

ELIZABETH. Gratitude?

WILLIAM. When we get the piano back. Could I have a shilling or two? This is something to celebrate. If you and Mrs Cunningham decide to join forces, nothing can stand in your way. Wait till I tell the boys about this.

He holds out his hand. She gives him some money from the wage packet. He gets his coat and hat, and goes to leave.

ELIZABETH. Can I expect you back before dawn? The police have got better things to do than haul you out of a fight or the river.

WILLIAM. You get yourself ready for Mrs Cunningham, she's your only hope.

ELIZABETH. She detests me.

WILLIAM. You'll think of something.

WILLIAM *exits*.

ELIZABETH *gets an idea. She gets a basin and starts
scrubbing her floor, with all the gestures of a back-sore
working-class woman.*

MAURA *returns. Before she can say anything –*

ELIZABETH. I'll show her I'm just an ordinary wummin, no
airs and graces. I'm as tough as she is.

MAURA. Mrs Cunningham's not coming.

MAURA *goes into the curtained bed-recess.* ELIZABETH
gives up on the working-class act.

ELIZABETH. Her pride got the better of her, did it.

MAURA. She's not in.

It's a chance for us to be alone with ELIZABETH; *when
she has nobody to impress, no public. There will be her
immediate response to where she finds herself – on her
knees – and how she gets herself out of that. As she empties
the basin she will no doubt be thinking of how to get her
piano back. But sometimes our obsessions weary us, even
disgust us.*

Scene Four

Wearing a coat over her night clothes, MRS BLACK *climbs
the tenement stair. It's a stairway to the void. At the top there is
nothing but a landing – and a door.* MRS BLACK *goes
through the door to the void. Behind the door she empties the
pail down a toilet, flushes it. Then she comes out and sits at the
top of the stairs.*

ELIZABETH *enters the kitchen from her bedroom, fully
dressed, and goes to her outside door, has a squint outside.*

She sees MRS BLACK *is there, goes to wake* MAURA – *who's in the bed-recess.*

ELIZABETH. Maura! Maura! Will you get up?

MAURA *wakes in dreadful fear and panic, gets up and into her shoes.*

MAURA. What time is it?

ELIZABETH. One.

MAURA. I'll lose my job. What will we do?

ELIZABETH *hands her the toilet-pail.*

ELIZABETH. Take the pail to the toilet.

MAURA. I don't need the toilet. Where am I going?

ELIZABETH. I have to speak to Mrs Cunningham.

MAURA. It's the middle of the night.

ELIZABETH. And I don't want Mrs Black to see me.

ELIZABETH *is pushing* MAURA *towards the door. She looks out her door to see if* MRS BLACK *is still there.*

She's still there. On you go. Distract her.

MAURA *starts up the stairs.*

MRS BLACK. Who's that?

MAURA. It's Maura.

MRS BLACK. Now don't mind me, you won't even notice me, no, don't bother your shirt tail about me, don't pay me the least notice. On you go; you go and do what you have to do, I'll just sit here and be no bother to anyone.

MAURA *disappears into the toilet.*

I'm like your mother, Maura. I'm a private person. I say, I'm a private person. I'll just sit here till I'm sure Mr Black has gone to sleep. I'll hear him. I come here because it's nice and quiet. Don't get me wrong, Mr Black hasn't said a word to me in eleven year, so the house is peaceful enough; but it's that quiet I'm frightened he'll overhear my thoughts.

Aye, it's good to come here and just sit and think out loud to myself. I got a letter from my son.

MAURA *reappears*.

MAURA. They found him?

MRS BLACK. They found him.

MAURA. Where is he?

MRS BLACK. He's at the seaside.

MAURA. When's he coming home?

MRS BLACK. Would you like a wee biscuit? I've got a whole big tin of biscuits hid away, Mr Black doesnae know a thing about. C'mon down with me.

MAURA. What if we wake him up?

MRS BLACK. I'm his wife; I can take as many biscuits as I want. I mind when you were a wee girl, Mr Black used to get you to sit up and beg for biscuits like a dug.

MAURA *knows* ELIZABETH *is probably listening*.

MAURA. I was the beggar in the family. It was me that get sent to the shops for food when they'd no money. I used to make my eyes look like big big pennies. Or if it was a shop that didn't know me, in the town, I'd point to what I wanted and make a hellish racket like I was a dummy, until they were all so embarrassed they gave me something to get me out of the shop. People would say to the shopkeeper, 'That would sicken you, so it would, to see that. She'll grow up thinking she only has to point to get something. And you give in to her, you encourage the selfish little article.'

MAURA *doesn't feel very pretty after re-enacting that*.

That was me. I used to sicken people.

MRS BLACK. Would you like some custard creams? I think I've got some custard creams you could have.

MRS BLACK *and* MAURA *exit into* MRS BLACK*'s house*.

ELIZABETH *goes out into the stair, and bangs on* MRS CUNNINGHAM's *door, extremely loud; using some implement she finds. Something disproportionate. Then she hears someone coming and retreats to her kitchen. Again we are alone with* ELIZABETH *for a moment; this time she seems weighed down, by the difficulty of what she's going to do. She has no piano to hide behind.* MRS CUNNINGHAM *comes to her door to investigate the noise, in her night clothes; finds her way to* ELIZABETH's, *knocking as she enters.*

ELIZABETH. Mrs Cunningham, you find me wide awake. Can I help you at all?

MRS CUNNINGHAM. Someone banged my door.

ELIZABETH. What is it you do? You look exhausted.

MRS CUNNINGHAM. I'm a munitions worker at Parkhead Forge.

ELIZABETH. A munitionette.

MRS CUNNINGHAM. I'm a turner. I turn shells. This week I start work at –

ELIZABETH. The rent strike seems to be holding.

MRS CUNNINGHAM. – seven which is why I look exhausted.

ELIZABETH. I've been wondering if you and your cohorts could get my piano back. They tell me it's being stored by the factor at his offices. Of course a piano can only be taken seriously in certain circumstances. It seems the sublime becomes the ridiculous in a room-and-kitchen.

MRS CUNNINGHAM *(describing a situation which has the suspense of breaking the law and the unknown consequences of that).* There are five hundred women on rent strike now, Mrs Quinn, and more of us every day. Mary Laird of the Glasgow Women's Housing Committee came to Parkhead Forge this afternoon; after she spoke, the shop stewards proposed a motion that any eviction of rent strikers would be regarded by those present as an attack on the working class as a whole, and one which would call for the most vigorous and extreme reply. As munition workers, it's illegal for us to go on strike; it's illegal for us to say we might consider going on strike. That's why we said the most vigorous and extreme reply. But have no doubts: if there are any more evictions, the workers at Parkhead Forge will stop producing the munitions we need to fight the war.

ELIZABETH. I will of course give you my full support.

MRS CUNNINGHAM. You'll join the rent strike?

ELIZABETH. I will personally speak to the factor on this subject. I will represent your case in the most vivid terms, believe me.

MRS CUNNINGHAM (*maybe has to drop her voice to achieve a factual sort of tone*). You see, if you want us to force our way into the factor's office and get your piano, I don't think I could ask the other women to do that unless you were to join the rent strike.

ELIZABETH. We don't seem to be understanding each other. I wonder if that's because as a materialist you see a piano as a piece of furniture whereas I think of it as a house of souls. Sometimes I hear a piano piece that sounds like the soul of a moment lost in time. Other pieces can be like, have you ever held a frog in your hand? The excitement, the fear. And sometimes a piece has a strange sort of presence, like the soul of sadness after the sadness has died and gone.

MRS CUNNINGHAM. It's two o'clock in the morning, Mrs Quinn, and I'm dressed for bed, which is where I would like to be right now. I'm still here because I have pretensions too. Just once I would love to read a poem about solitude in peace and quiet, or even in solitude, so I could understand what the poet is trying to get at. And I suppose it's pretentious of me to imagine I might have some control over my life, like where I live and what I get paid. I don't think we're so very different, you and me; but I'm afraid I can't help you unless you join the strike.

ELIZABETH. Am I too much of an individual for you, is that it? Do you want me to beg?

MRS CUNNINGHAM. Why would I want you to beg?

ELIZABETH. I still have my pride.

MRS CUNNINGHAM (*easily*). You have more pride than Marie Antoinette.

ELIZABETH. O, do I hear the working-class sneer. 'Does she think she is something?'

MRS CUNNINGHAM. I'm sorry, Mrs Quinn, I'm going.

ELIZABETH. I will not beg. Yes, I will beg. What have I got to lose, my pride?

She throws herself to her knees and crawls to MRS CUNNINGHAM.

Please. I beg you. I'm naked as a worm and I beg you.

MRS CUNNINGHAM. You won't embarrass me, Mrs Quinn. If you want your piano, all you have to do is join the strike.

ELIZABETH. I'll join your strike.

MRS CUNNINGHAM. Then I'll see what we can do.

MRS CUNNINGHAM *leaves.* ELIZABETH *gets to her feet. She's alone, alone with the feelings of what she's just done.*

ELIZABETH. I did not beg. I did not beg.

Scene Five

MRS BLACK *is cleaning the stairs. She finishes, puts down some newspapers to keep them nice till they dry.* ELIZABETH *goes out to see what's happening.*

MRS BLACK. I'm just cleaning the stair for them. I don't approve of them, I just don't want the close to get a bad name.

ELIZABETH. Nothing is greatly changed, Mrs Black.

MRS BLACK. You've joined their rent strike.

ELIZABETH. I can join their rent strike without being a part of it. Who's going to take any notice of a silly wee rent strike in some silly wee country? I'll rise above it.

MRS BLACK. I thought you had principles. How many are you expecting back?

ELIZABETH. I'm not expecting anybody back.

MRS BLACK. There was a good couple dozen of them when they set off with Mr Quinn. Have you got anything in for them, scones or that?

ELIZABETH. That would imply they were welcome.

MRS BLACK. You don't want to be sending to the baker's after they get here.

ELIZABETH. I don't think anyone who knows me will expect a scone, Mrs Black.

MRS BLACK *has followed* ELIZABETH *into the kitchen.*

MRS BLACK. I'm just looking at your kitchen and wondering what strangers might make of it.

ELIZABETH. The emptiness.

MRS BLACK. Do you want your drawers up on that pulley? There's not much you can do about the rest of it.

ELIZABETH. Listen. – Is that them?

MRS BLACK *goes to look out the window.*

MRS BLACK. Aye, that's them. Did you ever see the like? What a song and dance, and all for a flippin piano. O, and I can see Mr Quinn. You'd think he would know better than that. He's right in amongst them, raving away like a speaker at the shipyard gates.

ELIZABETH *retreats to a position where she can prepare herself for the ordeal ahead.*

Look at them. The whole street's hanging out its windows. What a show.

ELIZABETH (*preoccupied*). I just wanted my piano back, I did not expect to become a public spectacle.

MRS BLACK. Here they come, into the close. Now see and be nice to them.

ELIZABETH (*preoccupied*). I'll be perfectly pleasant.

MRS BLACK. Don't get on your high horse.

ELIZABETH. I always try and put people at their ease.

MRS BLACK. They're perfectly happy till you start putting them at their ease. All I'm saying is, whatever these people and their beliefs are, we can put that aside and be civil to them while they're guests in your house. I don't like people any more than you do but there's nothing for it. Are you ready?

ELIZABETH. It's at moments like this I wish my husband was beside me.

WILLIAM (*off*). We're here. We're here.

ELIZABETH. We could face the ordeal together.

MAURA. We did it. Look.

The piano enters in triumph, with WILLIAM *on top of it, bottle of whisky in hand. Two men –* BROGAN *and* McCORQUONDALE – *help to manoeuvre it into the house.* MAURA *arrives with them; she heads for the pulley and takes down the drawers.*

WILLIAM (*full of drink, fuller of life, in his element*). It has been a daze to end all daisies, I wish you could of seen it, Lizbet. Rosy wee cheeks of the factor nitswithstanding, when he threatened us with the metro polis, then, in the burds of the poet Shelley, rose we lick liars eftir lumber in unfangilable jumpers, we were moany, they could spew. O, the factor had a face like a spanked erse eftir, as though he wanted to say 'Whit was that fur?' And if he hud spake thusly we might have riposted, whit was it no fur? For in the heelin elation o victory we were as witty as a mink-coat. Notmahither, after the glaze of many bottles, we have returned, wagging our stories like a dug with two tales, and bringing you this joanna of the slums, this large but impecunious declaration of my love and adoration.

Silence.

MRS BLACK. You must be delighted, Mrs Quinn.

ELIZABETH. I trust your actions remained within the law.

WILLIAM. Yes.

MAURA. We just walked into the factor's office and asked for
  it.

BROGAN. Though Mrs Cunningham explained she could only
  guarantee the continued goodwill of the forty women
  present on condition he reinstated our piano.

ELIZABETH. I had hoped you would draw less attention to
  yourselves.

  *The jubilation of the victors is frosted by the reception
  they're getting, but only momentarily; the jubilation has a
  lot of momentum behind it and confidence in itself.*

MAURA. Can I introduce you to my two fellas?

BROGAN. Martin Brogan.

McCORQUONDALE. Pete McCorquondale.

MRS BLACK. I'll take whatever one you leave.

MAURA. You can't; you're married. She can't; she's married.

MRS BLACK. She wants the both.

BROGAN. She has to choose. Do you want animal spirits or
  intelligent conversation? In that case choose me. If you
  want to stroll in the moonlight while your fella tells you the
  infant mortality rate in each ward of the city, this year, last
  year, and eight of the nine preceding years, as well as the
  anomalies thrown up in the odd year, then
  McCorquondale's your man.

MAURA (*touched*). Infant mortality? Awww. And how do they
  actually work it out?

  Deafening silence falls on the company.

BROGAN. I hope you're just being polite.

MAURA. No, I'm really interested.

McCORQUONDALE. It's the number of infants that die within the first twelve months of life per thousand of infants born. Take the Cowcaddens. Last year the rate of infant mortality was one hundred and sixty-nine per thousand.

MAURA (*touched*). Awww. How many per thousand in the Gorbals?

McCORQUONDALE. A hundred and sixty-six.

BROGAN. The last person to take as much interest in infant mortality was Herod.

MAURA. And how many in Blackfriars?

MRS BLACK. I blame the weans. They're that wee. The least wee thing and – (*She snaps her fingers*.) that's them away. What can you do?

BROGAN. Can we have a drink?

WILLIAM *has a bottle of whisky.*

WILLIAM. As for myself, I am intoxicated already – with elation. I'm almost frightened with it – when I'm elated like this I always go too far, I'm liable to make a fool of myself. My wife on the other hand is unforthcoming in company, have no worries on her account. She expects everyone else to entertain her as I have done all our married life. Maura, will you fetch some glasses?

MAURA *starts to look for some glasses, though she knows they don't have any.*

Who's for whisky?

MRS BLACK. Whisky makes me kind of sick but I'll try one anyway.

McCORQUONDALE. Not me. I've my work to go to.

MAURA. What is it you do?

McCORQUONDALE. I'm a scavenger for the Corporation.

BROGAN. He needs to keep a clear head.

McCORQUONDALE. You can laugh but the statistics don't lie. The sewage workers and ourselves have saved many more lives than doctors.

MAURA. I wouldn't be seen dead with a doctor.

ELIZABETH. My father was in the same line as yourself, Mr McCorquondale. I remember the smell. Disinfectant and something else.

WILLIAM. That's three whisky glasses and a brandy glass for your mother.

MAURA. We don't have any glasses.

WILLIAM. We have a superfluity of glasses.

MAURA. No we don't.

WILLIAM. We have a reckless abundance of glasses. We have goblets of all descriptions. If this tenement were to suffer at the frenzied hands of an earthquake and be thoroughly shaken, all the broken glass in this house would form itself into a glacier of such a size that it would descend the common stair and deposit a moraine of glass halfway down the street. So do not stand there and tell me we have no glasses.

Silence.

BROGAN. I'll take mine in a teacup.

MAURA (*standing her ground*). Right.

BROGAN. If you have any.

MAURA (*standing her ground*). We've got one.

BROGAN. Is it cracked?

MAURA. Yes.

BROGAN. That's how I like them.

WILLIAM. Now; a song. If the people of this city are to be believed, every single one of them is the offspring of a shipyard worker and a music-hall turn – Mr McCorquondale, will you favour us with a comical song?

McCORQUONDALE *sits at the piano and plays the introduction to a song. Then sings.*

McCORQUONDALE.
Dear thoughts are in my mind
And my soul it soars enchanted
As I hear the sweet lark sing
In the clear air of the day.
For a tender beaming smile
To my hope has been granted
And tomorrow she shall hear
All that my fond heart would say.

WILLIAM. Very good, very good. I know very few songs myself but here's one I learned from a melancholy hussar as the day dawned in the Bay of Nice.

I am Captain Jinks of the Horse Marines
I feed my horse on corn and beans
And sport young ladies in their teens
Tho' a captain in the army.
I teach young ladies how to dance
How to dance, how to dance
I teach young ladies how to dance
For I'm the pet of the army.

Chorus.

I'm Captain Jinks of the Horse Marines
I feed my horse on corn and beans
And often live beyond my means
For that's the style in the army.

I joined my corps when twenty-one
Of course I thought it capital fun
When the enemy comes of course I run
For I'm not cut out for the army.
When I left home Mama she cried
Mama she cried, Mama she cried
When I left home Mama she cried
'He's not cut out for the Army.'

Chorus.

*And finish with a reprise of the first verse. Of course any
vaudevillian worth his salt would see the opportunities for
comedy-farting the song offers. 'I teach young ladies how
to ****. When the enemy comes of course I ****.' It's a
sort of song-and-fart routine.*

ELIZABETH. There was a time, Mr Brogan, Mr
McCorquondale, when I found my husband entertaining.
Now I am of the opinion that a pantomime is all well and
good once a year.

WILLIAM. And now, ladies and fence, would you be blind
enough to praise your spectacles – and jine me in a toot –
Oor piano.

ELIZABETH. Oor piano. Oor piano. Though I agree I cannot
argue with the accuracy of my husband's expression. The
piano which has traversed a city. The piano whose comings
and goings are the talk of the street. And now the working
class's piano – or should I say 'joanna'.

WILLIAM. When I said our piano, I was simply using a form
of expression.

ELIZABETH. You bring those men back to our house and
proceed to have a sing-song.

WILLIAM. I hoped you might join in.

ELIZABETH. How long have you known me?

WILLIAM. When I said our piano, Mr Brogan, Mr
McCorquondale, I meant to say that my wife and I wish to
extend our thanks, and what more after all can we give?

ELIZABETH. What a performance. Am I married to a comic
turn?

WILLIAM. Elizabeth, please don't –

ELIZABETH. Get out of my house, Captain Jinks.

Silence.

WILLIAM. Well, I'll be gingered. How my life has come to
this pass I do not know and I cannot conceal from you,
gentlemen, that I'm fair micshoogled. Remember the night

we eloped, Lizbet? It was a dirty wet night. In the taxi you gripped my arm like a small bird in a storm gripping a twig; and I swore I would never let you down. I've loved you so much it seems that every year I have got smaller and smaller. Perhaps I should leave now before I finally disappear.

He exits.

BROGAN. Where will I put my cup?

MAURA. I'll take it.

BROGAN. I've my work to go to now; I'm on a backshift.

MAURA *sees them to the door.*

MAURA. Do you go to the pictures much?

McCORQUONDALE. Yeah.

MAURA. I fancy the matinee tomorrow.

McCORQUONDALE. Big game tomorrow. Rangers versus Dumbarton. They're in seventeenth place.

BROGAN. We'll chap your door some of these days.

MAURA. I'll look forward to that.

BROGAN *and* McCORQUONDALE *exit.* MRS BLACK *picks up her basin of water, and goes up to the landing.* MAURA *manoeuvres the piano into the place it used to occupy, knocking over anything in the way.*

ELIZABETH. Look at it. It has been literally dragged through the gutter. O, I want to cut off my hair or something. I can still smell that scavenger. My father had the same whiff about him; the more disinfectant he used to get rid of the smell, the more stubbornly the smell clung to him. It was only the odd occasion my mother would have him in her bed. My poor father. O, he knew himself how bad he smelled.

Outside WILLIAM, *crossing the front of the stage, stops to look up at the wife he's leaving.*

MAURA. I'll go after him if you want.

ELIZABETH. Who?

MAURA. Your husband.

ELIZABETH. That night we eloped. What did I know? I was
fifteen just. In the taxi we swore not to fall into the bad
ways of other couples and to keep the promises we made,
whether our lives were short or long. I stank like a perfume
factory. I remember the feel of his coat against my cheek,
and how excited and afraid I was. He promised I would
never be poor again.

WILLIAM *exits*.

This stinking heat. The bins smell to high heaven. I'm going
to lie down.

MAURA. It doesn't have to be like this. You have a choice.

ELIZABETH *exits*.

Nothing's fated.

End of Act One.

ACT TWO

Scene Six

It's ten weeks later. In the raw cold of an early November evening, two MILITARY POLICEMEN *are too busy trying to keep their circulation going to have much to say to each other. One or two* PASSERS-BY *enter and are questioned by the* MILITARY POLICEMEN.

Inside, ELIZABETH *sits at a sewing machine; sewing. She's wearing a coat. Up the tenement stair comes* AIDAN QUINN, *dirty, cap down low over his face, out of breath and frightened. He stops outside the door of his house, considers knocking but doesn't. He continues up the stair to the landing and disappears through the door to the lonely void.*

Outside, MAURA *enters and is questioned by the* MILITARY POLICEMEN. *After she goes, we lose the exterior sounds; the* MILITARY POLICE *exit and now we are concentrating on* ELIZABETH. MAURA *enters and heads for the range to get a heat; she doesn't take her coat off and won't for the duration of the scene.*

ELIZABETH. Cold? I try not to let it bother me. Work work work, keep busy and keep warm.

ELIZABETH *picks up a big pair of scissors in one hand and her wedding dress in the other.*

MAURA. What are you doing?

ELIZABETH. I'm going to cut up my wedding dress. I was looking through some old things I've kept and decided it was time to get rid of some rubbish.

MAURA. No. Please. Whenever I see that wedding picture of you, standing beside your husband as though he is an archangel at least, and you scared but keen as mustard, my heart goes out to that fifteen-year-old bride and her mad, innocent heart.

ELIZABETH (*cutting the dress*). Be practical, Maura. I was thinking about the Belgian refugees and how they must be freezing, the poor souls, and then I saw my wedding dress and thought: well, rather than see it sit and rot in a box on top of a wardrobe. I decided to make them some gloves.

MAURA. Do you miss him?

ELIZABETH. Do I miss whom?

MAURA *doesn't answer. She goes to find a tin and a jotter she keeps in the press.*

MAURA. I'm scared in this house now.

ELIZABETH. O. Why?

MAURA. I don't know. I keep waiting for something to happen; then I realise it already has.

MAURA *finds somewhere to do her accounts. She has to keep a record of who has given her rent.*

ELIZABETH. Where have you been till this time anyway?

MAURA. I had to go and see one or two that were late with their rent.

ELIZABETH. Yes; she's the rent man now.

MAURA. We're withholding rent, we're not defaulters. Someone has to collect the rent and keep a record.

ELIZABETH. You count the money so often, anyone would think it was yours.

MAURA. I'm the treasurer for the tenement.

ELIZABETH. You count it twice a day.

MAURA. I can't afford to be out a penny.

ELIZABETH. You count it so much, the coins are sweaty. Do you pretend the money's yours? Look, she's blushing. You look like a miser counting her hoard.

MAURA (*furious*). You won't make me feel any more ridiculous than I already do. Yes I'm ridiculous: I've no money. So I work. I make money. The more money I have, the less ridiculous I'll look. (*She's shaking with anger, in this cold. Suddenly she feels the futility of it.*) You make everything ridiculous. You really do. I work all day then I shop, come home and cook, go out again to picket a tenement till all hours of the morning. And after all that, I come home to this. I don't know why I bother.

ELIZABETH. You must enjoy their company. You're never in.

MAURA. I look at the others and think, 'You've got homes. You've got men, children, you've got a reason to do this.'

ELIZABETH. You want your own home? (*No answer.*) You look at me and what I've made of my home and you want to emulate my success. (*Slight pause.*) That was a joke.

MAURA *puts the rent money away.*

MAURA. I'll heat you up some stew.

MRS CUNNINGHAM *enters.*

I'll be right with you, Mrs Cunningham.

ELIZABETH. Where are you going now? You're only just in.

MAURA. The family of scabs across the street has moved out; we have to stop the factor moving another family in.

MRS CUNNINGHAM. There's news, Maura.

ELIZABETH. Mrs Cunningham's probably wondering why we gave you such an Irish name, Maura. We called her after an aunt of hers that worked in the fur department of Pettigrew's. We had high hopes.

MAURA. What kind of news?

MRS CUNNINGHAM. The factor's taking eighteen of us to the Small Debts Court. If the court agrees that the rent owed should be regarded as debt, the court will get powers to arrest our wages.

MAURA. Go into our pay packets and help themselves to our money?

MRS CUNNINGHAM. There's twenty-five thousand of us on strike now. Look at it from their point of view.

MAURA. Take money out of our pay packets?

MRS CUNNINGHAM. They have to do something.

MAURA. You never said this could happen.

MRS CUNNINGHAM. I suppose they took legal advice. Used the best minds money can buy.

MAURA. We're going to lose?

MRS CUNNINGHAM. We have a few days before the case comes up in court, to drum up some support among the shipyard workers. Are you ready?

MAURA. It's freezing out there.

MRS CUNNINGHAM. Not much better in here.

MAURA. I don't know that I want to carry on if we're going to lose.

MRS CUNNINGHAM. We've got pea-and-ham soup out there.

MAURA. Who made it?

MRS CUNNINGHAM. Jessie McQueen.

MAURA (*to* ELIZABETH). I'll be in before one.

   MRS CUNNINGHAM *exits*. MAURA *stops at the exit*.

   I spoke to some military police outside. They say there's a deserter been going into people's houses and stealing food, so see and eat that stew.

ELIZABETH (*while sewing*). When I met your father I was little more than a girl. It made me shiver sometimes . . . he could see right through me. He seduced me. He was quite ruthless about it. Those first few precious months we lived like fugitives; I didn't care, I was with him. My ruthless lover. I was only just fifteen, though your father didn't know that, I was quite precocious. People gave us spoons; Mrs Hughes gave me a holy picture of Our Lady of Loreto to put in my missal, only I didn't have a missal. Yes they've grown hard, people; when I think of my childhood days, I could cry, so I could. The overcrowding was dreadful but

O, the people? – They were the friendliest folk you could
meet. They'd do anything for you; anything. These days,
they're a lot better off than we ever were, but these days it's
all self self self. When I think of my mother, working her
fingers to the bone and never a minute to call her own; and
always that cheery too. The few coppers she had to see us
through the week, but she still made me take soup to poor
auld Mrs Shearer that lived in the single-end next door. It
could be awful cold in the winter and poor old Mrs Shearer,
we'd give her coal, but would she burn it? 'I'm no worth
it,' she'd say. 'I'm only mysel', hen, and I'll no waste yir
Ma's coal. Naw, the cauld has got right deep into my bones.
Tell yir Ma I'm done. It's time to dig a hole and leave me.'
My mother would send me back and tell me to make a fire
for her myself, and I would try, but it was awful cold there,
some nights I didn't always wait to see if it had taken
properly. One morning I went in her house. Cold? It was
like being in an underground cavern underneath a black
black lake of ice. She wasn't even in her bed, Mrs Shearer,
she was lying out on the linoleum floor. I tried to wake her
but she was frozen stiff. Her eyes were like frogspawn.
O, the poor, the poor. You don't need to tell me my duty to
the poor.

MAURA *exits*. ELIZABETH *continues to sew*.

Scene Seven

Later, the same night. MRS BLACK *enters and climbs the
stair to the half-landing where the outside toilet is. A foghorn
blows*. ELIZABETH *goes outside her door, shouts up at* MRS
BLACK.

ELIZABETH. That fog is dreadful. It will sit there for a week,
that fog.

MRS BLACK. Are you talking to me?

ELIZABETH. After mass on Sunday I was speaking to the
Crichton-Stuarts and the young Miss Crichton-Stuart, wait

till you hear this, the young Miss Crichton-Stuart said, 'Look at that fog. It's thicker than a miner's piece.' That's typical of the proper upper class, the way she said piece rather than sandwich. 'It's thicker than a miner's piece,' she said. And they say the upper class have no fellow-feeling for the poor!

MRS BLACK. I don't know why you're shouting. Come up if you want to talk to me.

ELIZABETH. Go up there? I'm only talking to you out of pity.

MRS BLACK. You must be awful lonely in that house now your man's gone. I suppose I'm the only one that'll listen to you now.

ELIZABETH. I shouldn't even rely on that.

MRS BLACK. No. You should not.

ELIZABETH. No; what if you and Mr Black had a second romance?

Silence.

MRS BLACK. I couldnae stick another week in Buckie. They don't make you welcome. They all go out to sea and fish, leave you with nobody to talk to but him.

ELIZABETH. How's your son?

MRS BLACK. Still at the seaside.

ELIZABETH. How's the weather?

MRS BLACK. Blue skies.

ELIZABETH. Ice creams?

Silence.

MRS BLACK. You used to be an individual, of course. That was the great thing about you. You stood out. Now you're no different to any of the rest of them.

There's the noise of a tram and MAURA *enters from the street.*

MAURA. It gets right into your marrow, that cold. O, I wish I could hibernate. Maybe when I woke up, everything would be better. See? I would like to pretend too.

MRS BLACK. Is that the hard-faced bitch that drives families out into the cold?

MAURA. They were paying rent to the factor, Mrs Black. They left of their own accord.

MRS BLACK. They weren't wanted.

MAURA. That's right; they weren't wanted. They were traitors to their class.

MRS BLACK. I'll tell you who the traitor is around here. I'll show you a traitor.

The toilet door has opened behind her. AIDAN *is framed in the doorway.*

AIDAN. He's behind you, Mrs Black.

MRS BLACK *spins round and cries out in fright.* AIDAN *walks down past her.*

MRS BLACK. Aidan?

He walks down past ELIZABETH *and* MAURA.

ELIZABETH. Aidan.

MAURA *puts a hand over her mouth.* AIDAN *goes into the kitchen, followed by* MAURA *and* ELIZABETH. *All three are very polite, or very stiff anyway; as if they were all guests in this house.*

AIDAN. Any food?

MAURA. Not much.

AIDAN. What about the stew?

MAURA. I made that for her.

ELIZABETH. He can have it.

MAURA. That's yours.

ELIZABETH. Let him have it.

MAURA. She's stopped eating.

ELIZABETH. The less I eat, the stronger I become.

AIDAN. Does eating remind you of yourself too much?

ELIZABETH. Do you want it or not?

They're still very stiff. AIDAN *hasn't gone to get the stew.*

MAURA. Lock the door.

ELIZABETH. No.

MAURA. Do you want people to see him?

ELIZABETH. Nobody locks their door.

MAURA. They'd lock their doors if they had something to
    hide.

The penny drops.

ELIZABETH. Do you want to make an announcement?

AIDAN. Are we just going to leave it open?

MAURA. Have some stew.

AIDAN *has some stew.* ELIZABETH *and* MAURA *watch.*

ELIZABETH. You can't stay.

MAURA. You can't stay, Aidan.

AIDAN. Nothing is hung for long enough nowadays. Rabbit,
    traitors. Any more?

MRS BLACK *enters.*

MRS BLACK. I just came to make sure my eyes hadn't
    deceived me. What's the matter, Aidan, were you afraid?
    I'm sure there's plenty of them shite their pants; but they
    don't come home with the shite running down their legs.

ELIZABETH. He'll be gone by the morning, Mrs Black.

MRS BLACK. He better be.

ELIZABETH. I won't have another coward in the house.

MRS BLACK. I'll give him one night, no more. If he's not gone, I'll report him. They can come and take him to be shot.

MRS BLACK *leaves*.

ELIZABETH. Aidan, your father's gone.

AIDAN. Gone? When?

ELIZABETH. Three months ago.

AIDAN. Where is he? Did you make any inquiries?

ELIZABETH. You can make him up a bed, Maura. I hope, Aidan, you don't prove to be as big a traitor to me as your father did.

ELIZABETH *exits*.

AIDAN. Must be hard being a mother. All those emotions boiling inside you. I dare say we only see the tip of the iceberg. There's a lot more iceberg we don't see.

MAURA *gets the hurley-bed out from underneath her bed*.

MAURA. It's all made up. Sleep well. I should have been in my bed an hour ago.

AIDAN. Nothing you want to ask? You haven't seen me in four months.

MAURA *turns down the light, and starts to undress*.

MAURA. Nothing I want to ask, no.

AIDAN. How I survived? Why I've come home?

MAURA. You can't stay, Aidan.

AIDAN. It looks lovely, that bed. I could sleep for a year in that.

MAURA. Don't worry. I'll wake you.

AIDAN. I'll lie on the floor.

MAURA. The bed's made.

AIDAN. It's too clean. I'll dirty the sheets.

MAURA. Don't worry about it.

AIDAN. I stink. I smell like rancid butter.

MAURA. Take your shirt off. I'll wash your back.

AIDAN takes his shirt off. MAURA pours some hot water into a basin. She starts scrubbing him.

AIDAN. Ah yah. Not so hard. That's the scrubbing brush for the stair.

MAURA. You're a lot dirtier than the stair.

AIDAN. That's how I survived. Dirt. I got tired of begging and stealing and letting men touch me, and got a job as a smelly man.

MAURA. What does a smelly man do?

AIDAN. He works for a debt collector. Over in Dublin I worked for Powell's on Camden Street. You put shite on your coat and urinate in your trousers and stand on some dog-keech and put a dead rat in your pocket, it doesn't have to be a rat, anything that's decomposing, and the debt collector sends you to sit in someone's office until they pay up. No one lays a finger on you, they can't get close enough for gagging. You sit there in perfect peace and tranquillity. It's wonderful. It's like you disappear.

MAURA. Why did you come home?

AIDAN. Did I tell you I met the Devil on my travels?

MAURA. How was he?

AIDAN. Very bitter.

MAURA. I don't see why. Everything's going his way.

AIDAN. That's his nature. Even when things go his way – huge slaughter of young men, etcetera – he still finds something to complain about. (*After a pause.*) I'll be dead soon. You'd think there would be more to say.

Silence.

MAURA. It's . . .

AIDAN. What?

MAURA. Nothing. You could ask what's been happening here while you were away.

AIDAN. I see nobody washed those pots. Anything else?

MAURA. I took your job at the post office. They ask after you, have I heard anything. When things are going badly in the Dardanelles, Jack Webster gives me a digestive biscuit with my tea. We started a rent strike. They put the rents up too high, people couldn't afford it. It started in Govan, then they put the rents up here, Mrs Cunningham organised a petition. There's twenty-five thousand of us now. Women in Shettleston, Clydebank, Govanhill, all over. And it might all come to nothing.

AIDAN. I suppose if it does come to nothing, it's not the end of the world. The rents would go up, that's all.

She scrubs some more. She's crying.

Not so hard.

MAURA. Don't you think it's sad?

AIDAN. It's the rent. It's not a tragedy.

MAURA. It might all come to nothing.

AIDAN. What is it? What's wrong?

MAURA. Nothing. Nothing's wrong.

AIDAN. You're crying.

MAURA (*hardly able to speak for crying*). Raw meat, I feel like raw meat all the time, is that how I look?

AIDAN. No!

MAURA. I mean, am I pretty?

AIDAN. You're lovely.

MAURA. Yes, but am I pretty?

AIDAN. I don't know, I'm your brother. Here.

They hug. They both need someone, and they hold each other hard. Then he holds her away from him.

Will you tell me why you're crying?

MAURA. Just, nothing I ever do seems to come to any good. Give me the rest of your clothes, I'll go and wash them.

AIDAN. Have you got the key to the wash house?

MAURA. I can get it.

AIDAN. What if anyone sees you, washing a man's clothes?

MAURA. I'll tell them you're up here naked.

MAURA exits. AIDAN goes over to the piano, sits at the piano stool, wrapped in a sheet or blanket. He plays something short and piercing and sweet and tranquil. If it breaks anyone's heart, there is no sign of it. He finishes playing.

AIDAN (*to anyone who might happen to be listening*). Before the *Titanic* struck that fatal iceberg there was probably some piano player on board who hoped he could melt it by the sheer beauty of the music.

Scene Eight

There's a pulley up, with AIDAN's clothes on it. ELIZABETH enters, goes to her sewing table and starts cutting up her wedding dress and sewing. AIDAN appears. He's robed in sheets and a blanket, though it's freezing. He watches ELIZABETH sewing for a while.

AIDAN. What's that you're doing?

ELIZABETH. I'm making gloves for the Belgian refugees out of my wedding dress.

AIDAN. Can I see?

She holds up an example of her work. It's a tube with no hand, like a bandage.

ELIZABETH. It's an elbow-length evening sleeve. I keep picturing a wee Belgian girl that's blue with cold, and how her face will light up when she sees this.

AIDAN. It's an interesting theory, the survival of the fittest, but how would Darwin account for you, I wonder; or the survival of the Scots? The race with the worst lungs, livers, tempers, baldness, depression, wasting disease, cancers and piles – who require, for their daily survival, a quarter pound of sweeties, a large amount of batter with a small amount of something inside the batter, and oceans of sweet tea ladled out by a mother with angina who works her fingers to the bone then dies of heart failure at fifty-nine leaving behind three big sons who cry into their whisky at the funeral and fall into a morbid depression because they weren't fit to tie her varicose veins; the males and females of this race multiply themselves like lice in an overcrowded classroom of weans. What possible motivation could we have? Are we crabbit, ill-natured creatures that in our bitterness procreate, in order to inflict the ills of life and all her infirmities on generations to come?

ELIZABETH. You're so sentimental, Aidan. We didn't give you that much thought. Why don't you put some clothes on? Those clothes have been dry for hours.

AIDAN. I'm not going out in that fog.

ELIZABETH. Perfect weather to disappear in.

AIDAN. You want me to disappear?

ELIZABETH. You can't stay here. Surely you know that?

He can't or won't answer.

Someone with your level of intelligence. You can't hide for ever.

AIDAN. I've hidden this long. Strangers hid me.

ELIZABETH. They weren't ashamed of you.

AIDAN. I can't go back out there yet. I'm clean.

ELIZABETH. I'm beginning to wonder if you've come home with some fixed purpose in mind.

MRS BLACK. Is he still here?

MRS BLACK has entered (wearing a coat). She goes to take AIDAN's *clothes down off the pulley.*

I don't know how long I can stand it, knowing you're here in this tenement, it makes my insides want to crawl away. We're all afraid, sonny boy. We're all sick with fear. The boys at the front must be out of their minds with it half the time.

A COALMAN *enters the building chanting, 'Coal! Coal!' He's bowed under a heavy 112-pound bag of coal. He's got a leather protector on his back, a pouch of money to the front and his face is black with coal. The personality of the man is hidden behind the coal. Physically, it would be great if he was a wee man with skinny wee legs.*

ELIZABETH. He can't go anywhere without his clothes. Give him his clothes and let him disappear in that fog.

MRS BLACK. He's got no intentions of going.

The COALMAN *enters the kitchen.*

COALMAN. Coal, missus?

ELIZABETH. Whose coal is it?

COALMAN. McGuffey's coal.

ELIZABETH. Not the Coperative?

COALMAN. No.

ELIZABETH. I don't take Coperative coal. How much is it?

COALMAN. How much d'you want?

ELIZABETH. Tell me how much it is and I'll tell you how much I want.

COALMAN. It's 2/6d a hundredweight.

ELIZABETH. How much is a hundredweight?

COALMAN. 2/6d.

ELIZABETH. How much is a hundredweight in weight?

COALMAN. Quite heavy.

ELIZABETH. Wait till I see what I've got in my purse.

She looks in her purse.

I've got nothing in my purse. Aidan, see if there's any money in that press.

MRS BLACK. You're a fine-looking man, coalman.

COALMAN. I'm blushing.

MRS BLACK. I bet you have some fine strapping sons away at the war.

COALMAN. I don't think the army's so fussy as what they were. Their lungs are bad with the bronchitis and one a them has a disease of the urinary duct.

MRS BLACK. Still. They're away.

COALMAN. O aye . . . Christ, if they rejected all the rejects . . .

MRS BLACK. Her son's still here.

COALMAN. Is he on leave?

MRS BLACK. There's a word for what he is . . . but it's no a word I want to say in front of strangers, if you take my meaning.

COALMAN. They can fight too. The mary anns? They can be good at it.

MRS BLACK. This one's something worse than that. Here, I'll give you a minute; see if you can guess.

AIDAN. There's a tin here with a small fortune in it.

ELIZABETH. Bring it here.

MRS BLACK. Have you guessed, coalman? Eh, coalman, have you no guessed yet?

The COALMAN*'s got a job of work to do and he's got a hundredweight of coal on his back. He's an Atlas almost at the end of his patience.*

COALMAN. I'm waiting to see if you want some coal.

MRS BLACK. The Coperative coalmen refused to deliver to her. Will I tell you why?

ELIZABETH. How much coal can I get for threepence?

COALMAN. Threepence?

ELIZABETH. I'm not saying I'll take threepence. I want to see what threepence looks like first.

MRS BLACK. Eh? Will I tell you why the Coperative won't deliver to her?

COALMAN. Open your coal bunker.

The COALMAN *empties threepence worth of coal into her bunker, and* ELIZABETH *inspects it.*

How's that?

ELIZABETH. That? That's never threepence. That's twopence ha'penny if you're lucky.

The COALMAN *gives her another ha'penny's worth.* ELIZABETH *offers him a fiver.*

Right; have you got change of a five-pound note?

MRS BLACK. Will I tell you why the Coperative's men took against her?

COALMAN *starts giving* ELIZABETH *her change.*

ELIZABETH. These pound notes are filthy, what do you do with them?

COALMAN. It's the coal dust. It gets on my hands.

ELIZABETH. O, never mind, it can't be helped. How long will that coal last?

COALMAN. That coal will outlast all the works of man, so long as you don't set fire to it.

ELIZABETH. What if we burn it?

COALMAN. You'll be cold again before the morn.

He exits, followed by MRS BLACK.

MRS BLACK. Wait till I tell you why the Coperative's coalmen stopped delivering to her. Would you believe that, he's gone? He's ruder than you.

ELIZABETH. Can Aidan have his clothes, Mrs Black?

MRS BLACK. Go to the police and turn him in.

ELIZABETH. Why don't you do it?

MRS BLACK. If I do it, he'll get shot and you'll get the jail for harbouring a deserter. If you do it, he'll just get shot. You've got till nine; or I'll put on my good coat and walk to the police station with a good conscience, and a firm step.

MRS BLACK *exits with* AIDAN*'s clothes.*

ELIZABETH. Make a fire.

ELIZABETH *exits into the bedroom.*

AIDAN (*to* ELIZABETH). So you think I've come home with some purpose in mind? I'm going to stay here till you can't stand the smell.

Scene Nine

On the stair, MRS BLACK, *dressed in her best coat, enters, goes to the top of the stair and sits. She has* AIDAN*'s clothes, neatly folded, a small pile which she places on her knee.*

In the kitchen, AIDAN *is plonking away at the piano – 'Abide With Me'.* ELIZABETH *enters, reading; the way an actor might read a book on stage. She walks through her kitchen to the outside stair.*

ELIZABETH. Are you there?

MRS BLACK. You know I'm here.

ELIZABETH. I was just thinking. We have so much in common, you and me.

MRS BLACK. Like what?

ELIZABETH. We're both mothers.

MRS BLACK. Don't you go comparing your son with mine.

ELIZABETH. Do you remember when Aidan was a wee boy?

MRS BLACK. Aidan was a lovely wee boy.

ELIZABETH. Remember?

MRS BLACK. He never looked down his nose at me, I remember that.

Silence.

ELIZABETH. Are you determined?

MRS BLACK. If deserters can get away with it, then the whole thing's a mockery.

ELIZABETH *goes back into her kitchen, leafing through her book.*

ELIZABETH. Traitors, traitors, traitors. Here we are, Canto Thirty-four. The traitors are in the lowest circle of hell, frozen below the ice. They show through like pieces of straw trapped inside glass.

AIDAN *stops playing the piano. Then continues.* MAURA *enters the tenement stair from the street.*

MRS BLACK. Who's that?

MAURA. It's Maura, Mrs Black.

MRS BLACK. Where have you been till this time?

MAURA. Dalmuir.

MRS BLACK. Dalmuir? What's in Dalmuir?

MAURA. Beardmore's the shipyard. We went to talk to some of the men at the boilermakers' social club. It's tomorrow we appear in the Small Debts Court.

MRS BLACK. What did you talk to the boilermakers about?

MAURA. The phenomenology of mind.

MRS BLACK. You won't get a man that way. You won't
attract a decent man by talking about Hegel.

MAURA. Why are you wearing your best?

MRS BLACK. I told your mother. I'll report him if she doesn't.

MAURA. He'll get shot.

MRS BLACK. He'll get shot whatever happens. If you make
me go to the police you'll get caught harbouring a deserter.
Six months in the jail you'll get. You think your mother
could stand that? By the time you got out, the pair of you,
you'd have no house. You'd have to live on charity.

A foghorn blows.

MAURA. You must be lonely without your son.

MRS BLACK. You're never alone when you've got your
pride. You've no idea, the courage my boy has. You know
how, before a battle, the artillery fire shells at one another?
Well, one day the Cameronians were at Armentières, shells
screaming all around them; and the other lads in his
company, they had to wake my son up. He was sleeping like
a graven image. What do you make a that?

MAURA. You can't beat that.

MRS BLACK. That's like a story you'd hear at Sunday School
or the Boys' Brigade. He was sleeping like a baby. You're
the ones that are lonely, living with a deserter.

MAURA. Leave it to us. We'll report him. I've done enough
asking for charity.

MRS BLACK. I'll give you ten more minutes.

MAURA *goes down the tenement stair and into the kitchen.
She takes her coat and gloves off; then she gets her rent
book and rent tin to enter some more rent in it.*

MAURA. Who touched this money?

AIDAN. She used it to pay the coalman.

MAURA. That's not our money. That's the street's rent money. You could buy coal with the money I give you if you didn't spend it on sheet music.

ELIZABETH. I only took threepence.

MAURA. Nobody's allowed to touch this money except me. Do you understand?

ELIZABETH. The miser and his hoard.

MAURA. Are you going to pay it back?

ELIZABETH. How can I pay it back?

MAURA. You could go out and beg. You made me go out and beg.

ELIZABETH. If we'd known you'd go on about it for the next twenty years we would of let you starve.

AIDAN *finishes playing the piano*.

AIDAN. I'm afraid when your mother was a girl she swapped her conscience for a toffee apple.

MAURA. You can't get rid of a conscience. You know when you've done something wrong.

AIDAN. You mean there's always a place where your conscience used to be?

MAURA. The place where your conscience used to be is your conscience. It's your conscience that tells you, this is where your conscience used to be.

AIDAN. Imagine if I could touch my mother's conscience . . . Shouldn't one of you be going to the police . . . ?

ELIZABETH. Do you expect us to feel guilty?

AIDAN. Sending me to my death?

ELIZABETH. Aidan, you volunteered. You picked the regiment. You sailed to Dublin to join up. Then you deserted. Are you suffering from a weakness of the brain? – yes. Should you be taken out and shot for it? – that seems harsh but I am your mother.

AIDAN. Yes I volunteered; but you did talk about the war all the time. You read out reports of battles ad nauseam. We were up to our waists in mud and intestines. Finally I surrendered. I knew you'd rather have me dead than a post-office clerk.

ELIZABETH. If there are two words that make me shiver, those words are petty cash. I wanted you to get on in life. The war is a dreadful shambles but the men who fought at Ypres will never forget each other. It'll be a better recommendation after the war than the right school. If I pushed you to join up it's because I knew you lacked ambition.

AIDAN (*huge*). I was insanely ambitious. I had a yearning that consumed me like a hollow hunger for a pipe and comfy slippers; I had a burning desire to be the most mediocre post-office clerk in the entire history of the Anniesland post office; and when I think how my hopes will be ended by a firing squad of insurance clerks, it fairly makes my eyes water.

ELIZABETH. Get me my coat, Maura. I'm sorry, Aidan, but you shouldn't have come home.

MAURA *brings* ELIZABETH *her coat*. ELIZABETH *puts it on*.

AIDAN. You want to know why I came home? I wanted to be sure I hadn't made it up. When you're looking for the corner of a room to sleep in, you see the insides of too many homes and too many minds. Dumb spirits, and desires they only share with their dogs. And I began to wonder if maybe it had been really quite ordinary, my home, and I'd exaggerated it all. D'you remember the piano recitals, Maura, when we were young? We wrote invitations and delivered them. I would be about ten or twelve, what age were you?

MAURA. We don't have time to reminisce, Aidan.

AIDAN. We invited everyone in the close. You used to say, I want you to practise hard, Aidan; this is the only opportunity these poor people get to listen to classical

music. So I did practise hard, and the thing that created the
enchantment – the poor folk we invited actually came.

MAURA (*to* ELIZABETH). Go. Now. Please.

AIDAN. Mrs McManus and her ten children; Mr Dempsey
with the woman he claimed was his daughter; the Greggs.
First you would lecture them on the tragic lives of the
composers. The nervous prostration of Robert Schumann.
Or Puccini and his misfortune in a mad wife. Then you
would introduce me and I would astonish our little society
with a scintillating programme. Some scales, usually, as a
prelude, to show how serious I was, followed by 'The
Carnival of the Fairies', 'The March of the Dwarves' and
'The Arrival of the Brownies'. And d'you know why they
came, the Dempseys and Mrs McManus and the others?
They were being kind. One recital night, it was a summer
evening, I was leaning out the window listening to the
children shriek, I was as excited as all of them put together.
And I heard Mrs McManus call one of her sons in from out
the back. He pretended not to hear so she actually went out
the back to get him. She was livid. She hit him on the head
with her shoe and said it was time he learned he couldn't
just do what suited him, there was such a thing as
obligations; if Mrs Quinn had the kindness to invite us to
her home, it was small hardship to go and listen to the poor
woman, and if nothing else it might teach him to be grateful
for what he had.

For ELIZABETH *it's a moment of disenchantment. The fact
that she is staggered is buried in a small pause, before –*

ELIZABETH. That's. I'm not sure, Aidan, I see the relevance
of this to you deserting the field while still some distance
from the noise of battle. You know where I'm going, there
can be no element of surprise. If you're still here when the
military police arrive . . . well, no doubt I'll be to blame for
that.

ELIZABETH *starts to leave.*

AIDAN. It doesn't seem as loved as before, the piano. Did
something happen?

MAURA. Go.

ELIZABETH. We lost it. Your father made a spectacle of himself, bringing it back.

AIDAN. Is that why he disappeared?

ELIZABETH. You'll have to ask him.

AIDAN. I can't ask him: he's disappeared. Do you miss him?

ELIZABETH. He was a deceiver. The promises! Who says you can't live on promises? After we eloped I listened to him with my head tilted up like a bird being fed full of worms. Where were his promises lately? Where were his promises when I was starving for them?

AIDAN. You do miss him then?

ELIZABETH. Yes.

AIDAN. How much?

MAURA *goes to the sink, retches.*

How much do you miss him?

ELIZABETH. I was sucked up and carried off by a dark wind, when I met your father. I lost my mind in that wind. I couldn't see.

AIDAN. Yet even so, the piano was more important than he was.

ELIZABETH *makes to exit.*

AIDAN. What's wrong? Have I touched your conscience?

ELIZABETH. You've had your big scene, Aidan. I have to go.

ELIZABETH *leaves. She goes out onto the stair.* MRS BLACK *is putting on her gloves, ready to go outside into the cold.*

MRS BLACK. Is that you?

ELIZABETH. Yes, it's me.

ELIZABETH *is hoping* MRS BLACK *will stop her.*

I'd best be going, I suppose.

MRS BLACK. I was just getting ready to go and do it myself.

ELIZABETH. The sooner it's done, the sooner it's over, I suppose. Ah well, who are we anyway? Who'll remember our names in fifty years?

MRS BLACK. The starlings don't even have names. They just die and there's an end to it.

ELIZABETH. It's a hard world. You wonder what the purpose of it is.

MRS BLACK. Purpose? That's a laugh. Nobody gives me a moment's thought.

Like a dog ELIZABETH *hears something in this that we don't.*

ELIZABETH. How's your son?

MRS BLACK. Eh?

ELIZABETH. Any more word?

MRS BLACK. He's still at the seaside.

ELIZABETH. Still getting the lovely weather?

MRS BLACK. Aye.

ELIZABETH. That's great. November too.

MRS BLACK. O, it's unnatural.

ELIZABETH *starts to ascend the lonely stairs to the void.*

ELIZABETH. When's he coming home? We need some good news in this close. If we only had the consolation that someone in the tenement was happy.

MRS BLACK. It would be a tonic.

ELIZABETH. It would give us all a lift. When you see some of the soldiers in the street, the state of some of them. The limbless. Makes you think there's worse things than dying.

MRS BLACK. I've thought the same myself.

ELIZABETH. Is he dead?

MRS BLACK. No. He's not.

ELIZABETH. Why won't he come home?

MRS BLACK. He's eighteen, he says. Why should he come home? He says the shells in France were nothing to the silence in our house. He never wants to hear that silence again.

ELIZABETH *sits on the steps.*

I'm sick of sitting here.

ELIZABETH. Did you ever get a coconut when you were wee?

MRS BLACK. Once.

ELIZABETH. It was a hard job to smash it.

MRS BLACK. It was.

ELIZABETH. I could do that to my head some days. Smash it, then scoop the inside out.

MRS BLACK. Some of the thoughts that come into my head.

ELIZABETH. The same thoughts again and again.

MRS BLACK. You think, 'Is this the best I can do?'

ELIZABETH. The guillotine. The crowds. How brave I look. 'Let them eat cake.' Then my head drops into the basket of other heads.

Silence.

MRS BLACK. Wouldn't it be a relief for once to think someone else's thoughts?

ELIZABETH. It would.

MRS BLACK *holds out* AIDAN*'s clothes.*

MRS BLACK. Here.

ELIZABETH *takes them, starts downstairs.*

At least your son came home.

ELIZABETH *goes down the stairs, and into the kitchen.*

ELIZABETH. The piano was your father's wedding present to me. He couldn't afford it and I couldn't play it, though we led each other to believe the opposite.

She hands AIDAN *his clothes.*

Here. Go and get dressed.

AIDAN *goes to get dressed behind the curtained bed-recess.*

MAURA. You think we can keep him secret? There are nineteen females in this close and I know a lot more than I would like to know about every single one of them. There's not much left to the imagination in this tenement.

ELIZABETH *takes off her coat.*

ELIZABETH. Aidan?

MAURA. What will we do when we get out of jail? Where will we go? The convent for some soup?

ELIZABETH. Do you never stop turning things over in that head of yours?

MAURA. I have to do everyone else's thinking for them.

ELIZABETH. Aidan?

AIDAN. What?

ELIZABETH. Your father was awful proud of you.

AIDAN. I didn't know that.

ELIZABETH. I don't want you to die and break his heart.

ELIZABETH *exits to her bedroom.*

MAURA. You sleep as long as you like tonight, Aidan. Don't you worry about a thing.

Lights fade on everything except MRS BLACK, *in her lonely eyrie.*

Scene Ten

Outside, in the distance, lights in fog. Obviously there are
people holding these lamps and lanterns and candles but we
can't see them too clearly. MRS BLACK *is down on her knees*
washing the stair. She stops to look at the people and the fog.
Inside the kitchen, AIDAN *does the same.* ELIZABETH *enters*
from her room.

ELIZABETH. How can you see anything in that fog?

AIDAN. I can see all these lights.

ELIZABETH. Can you see any faces?

AIDAN. Just lights in the fog. Hundreds and hundreds of
    them. It's like a fog at sea, and knowing there's a huge
    whale out there.

ELIZABETH. The suspense.

    MRS BLACK *enters; and outside the lamps and candles*
    and lights melt away.

MRS BLACK. That's them coming back from the Small Debts
    Court.

ELIZABETH. Have you heard any news?

MRS BLACK. No. What about you?

ELIZABETH. How would I hear?

MRS BLACK. When I was out at the shops earlier I heard
    someone say there's five shipyards on strike today.

ELIZABETH. Five shipyards?

MRS BLACK. That's what they said in the butcher's.

ELIZABETH. That's about 30,000 men. All for the women in
    this street?

AIDAN. Who can say what's going on in that fog?

ELIZABETH. 30,000 men. How could that happen?

MRS BLACK. Ask Maura. She took a hurl down to
Beardmore's last night.

ELIZABETH. She took a tram away down to Dalmuir?

MRS BLACK. To bum up the boilermakers.

ELIZABETH. Away and find out what's going on out there.

MRS BLACK. Away you and find out. You're one of them.

ELIZABETH *goes out onto the stair; then she comes back
inside.*

ELIZABETH. Here's Mrs Cunningham; Aidan, go in the other
room.

AIDAN. I want to ask her about the strikes.

ELIZABETH. She could report you to the police.

AIDAN. She won't be able to find them. When the mob's out,
the police go into hiding.

MRS CUNNINGHAM *enters.*

MRS CUNNINGHAM. I'm looking for Maura. I lost her
outside the court. She never mentioned Aidan was home.

ELIZABETH. He's just arrived.

MRS CUNNINGHAM. Isn't your regiment in the Dardanelles?

ELIZABETH. Well, tell us the news. Is it true five shipyards
came out on strike today?

MRS CUNNINGHAM. More. At least 75,000 men, all in
solidarity with the women of this street.

ELIZABETH. How many outside the court?

MRS CUNNINGHAM. Who could say in that fog? But there's
25,000 women on rent strike now and there were plenty
speakers in George Square so they were expecting a crowd.
I heard Helen Crawford and Mary Barbour, and John
Wheatley, he gave a good speech.

ELIZABETH. Who?

MRS BLACK. Never heard of them.

ELIZABETH. Are they local speakers? It's dreadful how parochial we can be: I dare say if you mentioned these great names furth of Scotland you'd find nobody had heard of them. They can talk the local patois, I suppose, but that wouldn't count for much in London or New York or Buenos Aires.

MRS CUNNINGHAM. I'm sure the people in London and Buenos Aires have got good local speakers too. They might need them more than us, it's not as if we need anyone to rouse us to action. We only stopped to listen to them talking about solidarity because they were in the way, we had to fight our way through the crowd into the court. Then when we finally did, Sheriff Lee had a few private words with the prosecution and that was it. The prosecution was persuaded.

ELIZABETH. What about the law? Those men should have been at their work, building ships. There's a war.

MRS CUNNINGHAM. The law? How many policemen would it take to jail a hundred thousand of us?

MAURA. Mrs Cunningham.

MAURA enters, shawled in a huge Union Jack.

What are you doing here?

MRS CUNNINGHAM. I've been looking for you. Has something happened?

MAURA. Don't touch me. Stay where you are.

MRS CUNNINGHAM. Have you been assaulted?

MAURA. The military police are in the street. They're doing a house-to-house search.

Outside, two MILITARY POLICE enter and cross the stage, using torches to light the fog.

ELIZABETH. Aidan, hide!

AIDAN. Where?

ELIZABETH. Where?

AIDAN. Have they got dogs?

MAURA. They've got dogs in their van.

ELIZABETH. Go!

AIDAN. No, I don't want to be thrown to the dogs. There's nowhere to run to.

ELIZABETH. It wasn't me, Aidan. I'm not responsible for this.

MAURA. Of course not, you couldn't be held responsible for anything. You're a child. I did it.

MRS CUNNINGHAM. Maura!

MAURA. O, for crying out loud, don't look at me like that, it was only a matter of time before the whole street knew. This is a tenement. We can't hide our feelings here, never mind anything else.

MRS CUNNINGHAM. You hid your feelings from me well enough.

MAURA. After we won today, outside in the fog, I looked at you all and I thought you've all got things. You've got homes. You've got men. Look what I come home to.

ELIZABETH. I can just see you, Maura, in some circle of hell, cooking your own brains and eating them. Using your fingers to get into the corners of the skull, like it's crab.

MAURA. That's the problem with this family, we've got more imagination than we can afford.

Two MILITARY POLICE – *a* SERGEANT *and a* REGIMENTAL SERGEANT-MAJOR *burst in. They have assumed the deserter will be armed.*

SERGEANT. Don't move!

RSM. Out of the way!

SERGEANT. Don't speak except to answer questions.

RSM. Nobody make any clever remarks.

SERGEANT. We might not understand them.

RSM. And then we'll get annoyed.

SERGEANT. Are you Private Aidan Gordon Quinn?

AIDAN *comes to attention, salutes.*

AIDAN. Sir!

SERGEANT. I'm warning you, son.

RSM. We're under a lot of pressure.

SERGEANT. Don't move too quickly.

RSM. Nice and easy does it.

SERGEANT. Are you Private Aidan Gordon Quinn of His Majesty's Sixth Royal Munsters –

RSM. – currently fighting for their King and Country in the Dardanelles?

AIDAN. Yes, sir.

SERGEANT. You're under arrest, son.

AIDAN *is handcuffed.*

Right, Quinn. I take it this is your family.

AIDAN. Sir.

RSM. Say goodbye.

AIDAN *steps up to his mother. The* MILITARY POLICE *cover them with guns.*

AIDAN. Well, seems I'll be making the supreme sacrifice after all. I know I should have died far away without causing any fuss but I came back. It's hard to sacrifice your life if nobody cares.

ELIZABETH. You're making a mistake, Officer. You're taking the wrong person.

RSM. Who should we be taking?

ELIZABETH. There's nothing wrong with him. He's fine and healthy. You're amputating the wrong leg.

SERGEANT. That's enough. Move.

AIDAN *exits, followed by the* SERGEANT *and* RSM.
ELIZABETH *goes after them and is held back by* MRS
CUNNINGHAM *and* MRS BLACK.

ELIZABETH. Cut me out. I'm the disease. I'm the gangrene.
You've taken the healthy part and left the cancer. – O,
Aidan!

With MRS CUNNINGHAM *and* MRS BLACK *on either
side of her,* ELIZABETH *goes back into the house where*
MAURA *is the only one left. She is still shawled in the
Union Jack. It seems bombastic now. She takes it off,
ashamed.*

Look at her. Look at that face.

MAURA. I don't think I can stand any histrionics.

She goes to wash some pots.

ELIZABETH. You think we should avoid any melodrama?
You just sent your brother to be shot.

MAURA. Make of it what you will.

ELIZABETH. Make of it what you will? She's mad as a
monkey. She's clean insane.

MAURA. You made me like this.

ELIZABETH. O, I'm to blame? You lay awake at nights
thinking, thinking. Could you not just go to sleep and dream?

MAURA. You stole my dreams. I lay awake worried sick,
thinking about that piano. I can't describe the panic I feel
when I look at it. I look at it and I completely panic. I'm a
wreck. Some of the strings still work but I don't know
which ones. I never know what noise I'm going to make.
Sometimes it sounds perfect and I get the shock of my life.

ELIZABETH. How can I live here now? It's like going to a
dance in a big empty hall. Nobody there you want to see. A
piano nobody can play and – What's that smell? What's that
smell?

MRS CUNNINGHAM. What smell?

ELIZABETH (*she points at* MRS BLACK). It's you. The disinfectant smell.

MRS BLACK. It's disinfectant. I've been cleaning the stairs.

ELIZABETH (*to* MRS BLACK). Get out of here. Get out of my house!

She backs MRS BLACK *out of the kitchen and up the stair.*

You do it on purpose. You want to bring me down to the same level as the rest of you and you don't know any other way to do it.

MRS BLACK. I like to keep the stair clean so people don't give us a bad name, that's all.

ELIZABETH. You want us all to be equal. Well, I've had enough, I'm. – O, Daddy. I'm sorry. Will you help me, please?

She goes back down into her kitchen and goes to get a poker.

Traitor.

MAURA. How many have you betrayed? She wouldn't go to chapel with her father, even when she was seven. You made him go to eight o'clock mass, you went to ten in your nice Sunday dress. She wouldn't sit on his knee, she wouldn't let him brush her hair unless he bribed her.

ELIZABETH *attacks the piano with the poker. She smashes the back panel and makes an unholy racket with the strings. After she finishes, she sits on her piano stool.*

ELIZABETH. Don't listen to her, Mrs Cunningham. We adored each other, me and my father. There was nothing like it. I let him brush my hair sometimes. He knew he smelled bad himself, he knew nobody could like it. No no, I never betrayed anybody; I refused to learn how to be poor, I've been true to my father every day of my life.

MRS CUNNINGHAM. They say it's good for your character to be raised in poverty. I suppose it is all right if you get rich.